Digressions

Digressions
Ian Duhig
Philippa Troutman

Smokestack Books
PO Box 408, Middlesbrough TS5 6WA
e-mail: info@smokestack-books.co.uk
www.smokestack-books.co.uk

Text copyright 2014, Ian Duhig, all rights reserved.
Illustrations copyright 2014, Philippa Troutman, all rights reserved.

Cover image: Philippa Troutman, *The Word Minotaur*

ISBN 978-0-9927409-7-9

Smokestack Books is represented
by Inpress Ltd

Contents

The Poem (burn and Ink)	10
Blockbusters	11
Lockean Keys	13
Cock (monotype, mixed media)	14
Asterion (monotype, pen and ink)	15
Calculating Chance	16
Echo Chamber Music	18
The Copyrighter's Song	19
Stones	20
Bert Lloyd	21
City of Troy (drypoint, chine collé, brush and ink)	22
Indirections	23
Li Xiaodong's Maze	25
The Word and the Bull	26
Rose Window (monotype)	27
Fall	28
A Double Bolide	29
The Marbled Page	30
The Black Page	31
Untitled (brush and ink, typewriter)	33
Combat Gnosticism	34
Dives and Lazarus	35
Big Ends, Little Ends	36
Sanctuary (drypoint, collage, mixed media)	37
Shapeshifting Ghosts of Byland Abbey	38
Mr Humphreys and His Inheritance	40
Gnostic Hymn	41
Line Please	42
Helthwaite	43
Blind Jack (drypoint, drawing)	45
The Ballad of The Blind Man's Road	46
Merlin (collage of *Tristram Shandy* text, drawing)	48
Which Reminds Me	49
Widow Wadman (pen and ink)	50
The White Page	51
Hobbyhorse (mixed media)	52

Lost Chapter	53
Notes and Acknowledgements	57
Tricorn (mixed media)	58
Afterforeward	59

Cover: *The Word Minotaur*
(screenprint, mixed media including *Tristram Shandy* text)

Inside front cover:
Marbled Meteor (Suminagashi experiment)

Inside back cover:
Fall of Light (Suminagashi experiment)

Blockbusters

> 'He lives in Leeds, completely out of the literary world.'
> John Freeman, ex-editor *Granta*

> 'Thrillers like *The Da Vinci Code* are key indicators
> of contemporary ideological shifts'.
> Slavoj Žižek, *In Defence of Lost Causes*

For what might break a writer's block that grips
my pen as if King Arthur's sword,
I quest through bookshops of My Lady Charity
in Urbs Leodiensis Mystica,
completely outside Freeman's (as most) worlds,
where locals speak blank verse (says Harrison);
Back-to-Front Inside-Out Upside-Down Leeds,
according to the Nuttgens book I bagged
along with authors offering keys to open
secrets of iambic pentameter,
how it's a ball and chain, a waltz – but best,
in Žižek's windsock for the New World Order,
Gnostic code imprinted by five feet
that lead us to a grail Brown liquefies
as Shakespeare melts to decasyllabics
like congealed saint's blood in a Naples shrine.
Brown quotes from Philip's Gospel where it suits
to build on Rosslyn Chapel's premises
vast hypophetic labyrinths in the air,
yet blind to masons' mysteries below,
who carved among the seven virtues greed
with charity being made a deadly sin...
The world was made in error Philip wrote –
Savonarola, in *The Rule of Four*
(another blockbuster from Oxfam's shelves)
is made to quote 'the Gospel of St Paul' –

does what seems error hide a secret truth?
What if 'Paul's Gospel' really did exist?
What if it was some long-lost Gnostic text
thrown on the Bonfire of the Vanities,
so seen there by our zealot's burning eyes,
a road-map to the Holy Grail now ash
but seen there by our zealot's burning eyes?
My back-to-back looks on a blind man's road
that draws a straight line north past Wilfred's city,
Shandy Hall then on to Lindisfarne
whose monks St Wilfred had been sent from Rome
to knock back into line from toe to top,
their sinful tops being 'Simon Magus' tonsures,
named for that gnostic heresiarch
a dog denounces in St Peter's Acts,
where Peter raised smoked tuna from the dead,
explained his crucifixion upside-down,
then how God's Kingdom might be found on Earth:
Make right your left, back forwards, low your high
then, in a flash, like Paul, I saw the light
through Peter's apophatic paradox
as if from some impacting meteorite
that would become Von Eschenbach's stone grail,
the grail that I had thought my writing block:
it freed my pen like Arthur's sword to write
this poem backwards, as Da Vinci might.

Lockean Keys

1
The signal box at Coxwold
serves a line that isn't there,
connecting nothing with nothing,
thin air with thinner air

but its *trains of ideas*
(the phrase is Locke's)
take you to – & – & –
past Coxwold signal box.

2
An Irish bull, an English cock,
a cat, a mouse, a tree, a clock;
an abbey's stones, its changing faiths,
a knife, a book, shapeshifting wraiths;

a hobby horse, a maze called Troy,
a starry name, Didius' boy
whose meteorite broke the mould
of Ptolemy on a Yorkshire Wold.

3
A poem is a meteor
Wallace Stevens wrote,
one of his lines
I often quote
or pass off as mine
to strike the poet note.

A meteor turns to fire
in the course of its flight;
one crashing to Earth
is a meteorite.
That is the poem I'm here to write.

Calculating Chance

> 'An Irish bull is always pregnant'
> *John Pentland Mahaffey*

Accidentally misconstruing the word 'Sternomancy'
in Creech's version of the Third Book of Pantagruel,
I took to calculating chance via *Sortes Shandeanae*,
sliding a knife between the pages of my 1783 Sterne
like artists seeking a name for dada in the dictionary.

I first turned a warning: *Go not further into this thorny
and bewildered track, intricate are the steps! intricate
are the mazes of this labyrinth! intricate the troubles
the pursuit of this bewitching phantom KNOWLEDGE
will bring upon thee...* too late. I was already bewitched.

I used the knife again: *If I thought you were able to form
the least judgement or probable conjecture to yourself
of what is to come in the next page, – I would tear it
out of my book...* But I knew the myth of authorial intent.
On the third time of trying, I found a voice: *Speaking*

of my book as a machine... it reminded me of Calvino,
making the tarot 'a narrative combinatorial machine'.
I knew I was on the right track, especially when I read
Though man is of all others the most curious vehicle,
hobby horse centaur. Rider, like the tarot deck's name.

Ridden too, interchanging their atoms as I interfaced
with Sterne. I read *as sure as I am I and you are you –
and who are you? said he. Don't puzzle me; said I...*
My skin grains like calfskin binding; my speech fills
with dashes and aporias, my lungs with ink like blood.

The calfskin grows into an Irish bull. I grow its head,
a minotaur in a labyrinth I built, stalked by this poem.
I feel its blade sliding down, along, between my ribs,
then rounding on my swollen stomach like a scalpel
rehearsing its lines before making the Caesarian cut.

Echo Chamber Music

> 'More binds Walter Benjamin to Walter Shandy
> than their common first name.'
>
> Samuel Weber, *Benjamin's -abilities*

Walter Shandy thought *nomen est omen*,
so tried to name his son for a great man
but providential stuttering foiled his plan.
True art is one, thought Walter Benjamin.

Walter Shandy's clock undoes his heart.
Benjamin damned dada for destruction
of the aura which distinguishes true art
by the means of its own art's production.

Rhyme also reproduces, but in the mind.
Dada echoes the sound of the new gun:
what the thunder said in World War One,
stuttering. A poem is a clock designed

to stop, I've heard. In this respect, it's like
a man; yet if men and clocks both strike,
clocks or poems won't try to stop another,
as, even gently, Walter Shandy's brother.

Benjamin and Shandy share a first name
which, oddly, means the ruler of an army;
that Weber doesn't mention this is barmy,
but I'm a poem. What I think is all the same

The Copyrighter's Song

He's Dante's thief, shifty between *I*s,
so many serpents shedding selves,
lying as that is how he goes to work

for *Plagiarus* also means 'seducer':
sticky fingers between your sheets,
stolen kisses, lip service as unpaid

as Hell or Dante's debt to Ibn 'Arabī
whose Sharia takes thieves' hands
but not their letters, their signatures,

not yours too truly, all too faithfully,
getting under skin enough to pass
for you, to be incubus in your pen,

contraceiving what you most love
for one-night stanzas in your mask:
you won't know you've got the clap.

Stones

My conceptual version
of a Cornelia Parker artwork
involves a 1783 edition
of the *Collected Sterne*:

an imaginary meteor leaves
a real scorch mark
the shape of a roast chestnut
on Phutatorius' chanticleer

as the flies of his breeches
lie open to interpretation
like the Gates of Horn
or the doors of perception.

Bert Lloyd

Inventing people like 'Tom Cook'
as sources for a song
in versions Bert himself cooked up
was ethically wrong,

but if once Reynardine flashed eyes
and then for Bert flashed teeth,
yet Reynardine would recognise
his passion underneath.

Which line was written by Bert Lloyd
the song won't care, of course,
nor we who plays the Mari Lwyd
or who the hobby horse.

When Burton denounced plagiarism,
Sterne did so in turn –
but in the words he stole from Burton –
one reason we love Sterne.

Down by the Salley Gardens
Yeats plagiarised Anon:
the nameless same Bert credited
in blank masks he put on.

Ghost-writing for his unborn ghosts
perfected Bert's own style;
his Lorca beats most other versions
by a country mile.

A mark of Nature, we've been told's
abhorrence of a void;
it's natural I sound like Bert,
the polyphonic Lloyd.

Indirections

I: Wrong Turn

> 'Later, the language of the people, which up to then had been known as Trojan or Crooked Greek, was called British.'
>
> Geoffrey of Monmouth, *The History of the Kings of Britain*

Askew from Skewsby, but not too far;
a minute's digression from Shandy Hall
(though harder to find than Shangri-La)
they built a new Troy without any walls
or signposts, as if to thwart invasions;
remaining unmarked on motoring maps,
this smallest of all Britain's turf mazes
was never designed as a tourist trap,
but turns like a sonnet to trap Old Nick
as he can only move in a straight line,
the locals say, who might seem thick,
still shy of strangers and their designs –
but if in the end they choose to speak,
it sounds like Trojan, or Crooked Greek.

II: Doubling Back

'Our language can be seen as an old city: a maze of little streets and squares... In the actual use of expressions we make detours.'

Wittgenstein, *Philosophical Investigations*

A stranger will ask, *Why the 'City of Troy'?*
The answer to this turns into a maze –
it's lost in translation; a turn of phrase
unwinding from the old Welsh Caerdroia,
where Droia was 'Troy' but 'Turns' as well...
so runs the web's unByzantine explanation.
But does Caer mean 'City'? Isn't it 'Castle',
as in Caernarfon, whose Byzantine walls,
like Byzantium itself, are also translations,
Roman into Greek – still all Greek in Wales,
as its conqueror's words to local Britons
who he made slaves, working like Trojans,
now called 'Welsh', 'English' for 'Strangers'
(from invaders' *extraneus* and *etrangiers*)?

Li Xiaodong's Maze

I'm told the Year of the Horse is good for poets.
I toast the new one now at the Royal Academy
with architects and poets counterpointing arts,
all gathered to make an exhibition of ourselves.

Chinese hosts at feasts once floated wine bowls
down garden water mazes to inspire their poets;
our host's bowls are made of a sense of space:
architecture's frozen music is the air we drink in.

Stanza's Italian for room; in Arabic, it's house.
A poem is a house that is trying to be haunted,
but poets aren't like architects so much as rats
building mazes from which they'll try to escape.

Since demons can only travel in straight lines,
lose yours in Li's maze here; its secret rooms
are this poem's forgotten stanzas, ghost drafts
still fleeing their own demons. To absent friends.

The window in Li's maze's shows us dancers:
light fantastic paths wind up in another garden,
a pool of pebbles worn smooth as old lullabies,
a mirror wall an echo chamber for their silence.

Which way now? In English, he who hesitates
sits on the fence; in Chinese he rides the wall.
Li's hazel walls remind me of Jansch's horses,
the ostler's son Keats' choice: doctor or poet?

Frank Lloyd Wright said doctors bury mistakes:
architects can only advise clients to plant vines.
The fruit of my vines fill the bowl I now float down
this poem's water maze toward you. Good health.

The Word and the Bull

Our New Age Christian neighbour's round;
who once was lost, but now is found.
His wine and card both gifts from Chartres,
its labyrinth, he says, more than art:

mere earthly mazes' paths get crossed;
to left or right we've always lost –
God's labyrinths have just one road through,
he says. But is this wholly true?

He's lost the thread that unwinds for
the half-true, crossbred Minotaur,
whose maze was all the world he trod
because his father crossed a god.

Just up the road in Hadrian's Wall,
its Mithraeae still show us all
where Minotaur and sacrificed
would cross the paths of Jesus Christ.

With Mithras born on Xmas Day,
'X' marks the spot, I do not say;
a silent, two-faced hypocrite,
I'm his God's Laodicean spit.

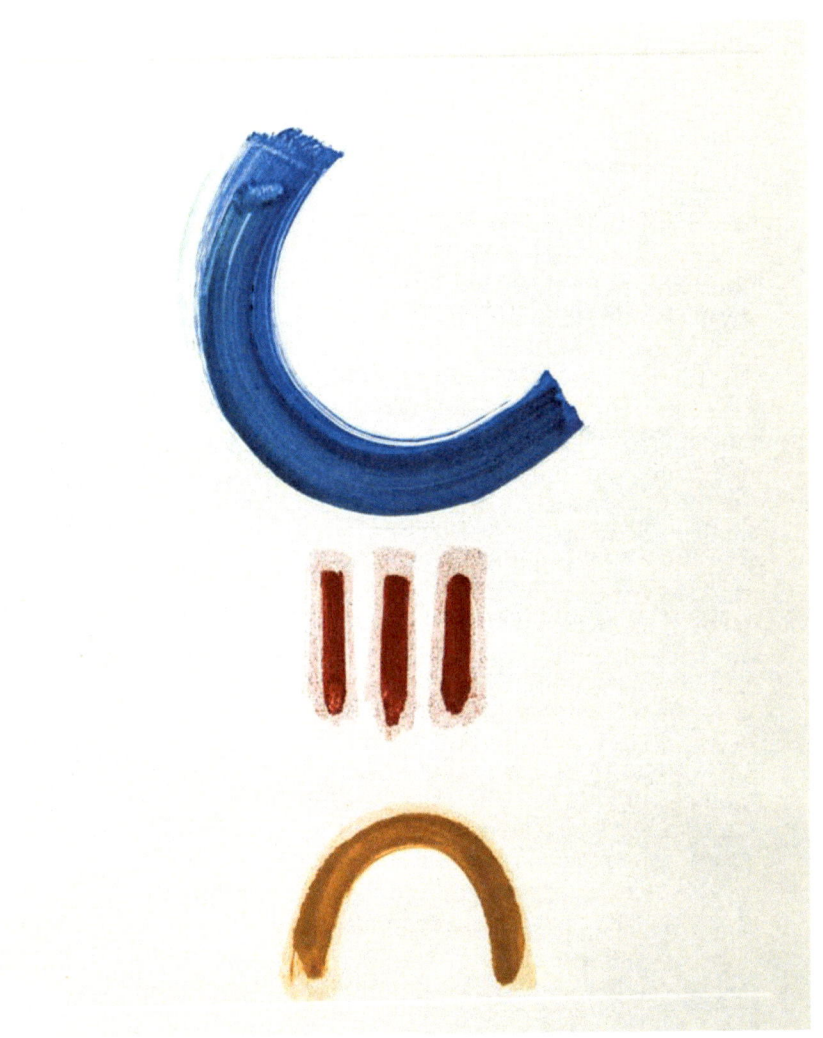

Fall

Bewildered leaves
Fall on our lives.
Northern Autumn,
Northern Auden.

Since that tree fell,
from Shandy Hall
you're able to see
the ruined abbey,

ancient North light
long since gone out
on the Cistercians
in their decadence;

its Rose Window
so overblown, below,
the cupped capitals
spill down the walls;

ivy, vine leaf scroll,
uncumbered corbel,
in limestone braille
praising Byland's fall,

prey to King Henry
blinded by family.
Leaf, life and tree
fell like his dynasty

cursed by Raftery,
whose *Annraoi Rí*
ruled with his rod,
his one-eyed god.

A Double Bolide

Scientific dating tests connect the Hambleton pallasite
from Kilburn's White Horse with the 1783 Great Meteor,
a brilliant double bolide heard then exploding over York.
In another report of the event in the London Magazine,

an officer on a British warship moored north of Ireland
related that a little time after he first noticed the meteor,
'in the north-east quarter, he saw it moving back again,
the contrary way to which it came' in Sternean fashion.

Perhaps it presaged that year's Irish stage premiere:
Tristram Shandy: A Sentimental Bagatelle in Two Acts.
This adaptation, playing up patriotic aspects of the text,
was by Leonard McNally, whose book on the law fixed

our criminal trial standard of 'beyond reasonable doubt'
indebting future civil libertarians to this Dublin barrister,
a man who came to play many parts during his own life,
with this starring role only coming to light after his death:

McNally was a founding member of the United Irishmen,
informing on them for pay and, when acting as counsel
for the Rising's leaders, he collaborated with the Crown
to guarantee their convictions beyond reasonable doubt.

McNally was also the lyricist of that sentimental ballad
'Sweet Lass of Richmond Hill' which invented the cliché
a rose without a thorn and was a favourite of George III's
since its first airing in the year of the French Revolution.

O the pikes must be together by the risin' of the moon
declares one sentimental ballad about the Risin' of '98,
reminding me that Sterne coined the word 'sentimental',
how his name meant star in the Hanoverians' language.

The Marbled Page

For Aristotle, marble's motley
trapped gobs of first matter,
like meteorites, from Creation:
God as he dreamt up Fortune.

Book-makers painted Her face
on gum-dragon, alum, ox-gall,
flea-seed and carrageen moss;
it moved on these new waters.

With such ink, a pen feathers;
a quill puns itself into a swan.
The twig in its beak-nib bursts
into marbled leaf, marbled tree.

Its bark is our word for book,
this book our vicar's machine;
he trusts in its divine engine
for providence of sentences.

His next sentence turns astern,
spilling its time, as the puffball
of our vicar's name spills stars.
Every star goes forth and back,

goes back and forth, multiplies
like spiral galaxies, or live cells
combining in a microscope lens.
Art is the matter; matter, the art.

His wild words whirl and whorl,
spinning from Fortune's wheel.
A book-maker clears his throat,
gobs into the marbling trough.

The Black Page

Lile ba léir é,
an Irish song runs,
ba linn an lá,
a chorus of guns;

it might go King Billy's
or King James' way:
The lily shone clear
and we won the day...

'*Lilliburlero*',
signature tune
of Tristram's mild Uncle,
Toby *a rúin*.

Orange the Lily O –
Protestants black,
in the tongue of Sterne's birthplace,
behind his back.

In the silence of Irish
so locked in the pen,
dubh might mean black,
but not like black men:

only the Devil's *dubh*,
Father of Lies,
Lucifer, Satan,
Lord of the Flies.

This High King of Ink
drew straight as a dye
in hatching a portrait,
a sin or a lie;

he'd prove black is white,
that rhyme has a reason
in Sterne's tongue where Irish
religion spelt treason.

But Yorick's black page
is kind to a blot
that might be true
or that might not.

past,
(strikit
so as to
—(drop
'Twas in
tears.—W
the cook-m
who was sc
with it.—Th
Now, as I
constitution
tion of the w
distribution a
time to come
of this strok
your attentio
pages toget
of the wor
I said,
should
men
tion
betwixt these an
for my own part,
suffice to affirm, t
lutely deny the tou
are for it) has the q
a smarter stroke, and
upon the fancy, th
times get rid of.
—I've gone a littl
us only carry it back
hat.—'Are we not here
There was nothing in the

Combat Gnosticism

Campbell's term for war writing born
of a gnosis only being there can earn:
I witnessed it once from old soldiers
in a poetry workshop at Age Concern.

They'd lost that battle with the word,
believing too much best left unsaid
to me, any other audience and pals
now three score and ten years dead.

*How many old soldiers does it take
to change a lightbulb?* Asked one.
You can't know if you weren't there!
They all fell about. Now they'd won.

Relaxed, they began letting it out
into grey shades of afternoon light,
into words they feared betrayed it,
and I learned why they were right.

Dives and Lazarus

Vagrants' graves stir by the Poorhouse
as midnight prayers to the God of Hosts
wind around the obelisk in Market Place,
a Cleopatra's needle for bone-lace ghosts.

Dead hand-loom weavers spin and reel
as sin-eaters flinch from witch-smellers;
the Risen of the North surround a Dean
who sold bells for wine to fill his cellars.

Still nursing his plastic two-litre bottle,
a squaddie suicide featherstitches past;
his Buckfast Abbey and tequila cocktail
the local police have nicknamed *Killfast*.

His khaki threads on the obelisk's bobbin
could unwind now by candlelight to tell
the miles from his child's bed to Babylon,
feet to Ozymandias, inches to the Skell.

The Clock warns *'Except ye Lord keep
ye Cittie ye Wakeman waketh in vain';*
vain the fool waking those not asleep.
The Skell gathers itself to drown again.

Big Ends, Little Ends

A character in Bradbury's *To The Hermitage*
satirises the idea of the death of the author
by inventing a theory called *Postmortemism;*

he applies this during a discussion of Sterne,
whose stolen body wound up under the knife
of the anatomist Professor Charles Collignon.

To Cole, Professor Collignon was an anatomy:
*a perfect skeleton himself, a walking shadow,
all flesh wasted* – like Sterne in life and death.

Sterne's skull later turned up in a churchyard,
crown sliced off in the fashion of anatomists
or the breakfaster addressing the boiled egg,

supposedly identifying him but doubt remains:
Sterne was often Yorick and Tristram Shandy.
Perhaps he was Professor Collingham as well.

Any line drawn to separate is a trouble in itself;
in wars between Big-Endians and Little-Endians
one Emperor lost his life, and another his crown.

Chop-fallen laughter from Coxwold churchyard
since the reinterment of these disjecta membra
could be Sterne's or from another osteo-collage,

like Ben Bulben's Yeats from Roquebrune bones,
with cold-eyed hobby horsemen passing by both.
At the end of his novel starring the Postmortemist,

Bradbury adds in its Note: *Books breed books;*
they go on, generation after generation, the flesh
of pages melting, bone shells of words endless.

Shapeshifting Ghosts of Byland Abbey

In a note to his *Twelve Mediaeval Ghost Stories,* M.R. James
explained a monk of Byland Abbey had collected them locally,
written them down then hid them in an unrelated manuscript.
He noted this text's difficult handwriting, its *'refreshing'* Latin,
local colour, confusion, incoherence and undue compression.
A moralising Christian editorial hand was much in evidence.

In one of the tales here, a man meets *something like a horse,*
one of the common supernatural incarnations of the Gytrash,
which turns into *a whirling heap of hay with light at its centre.*
Changing into human form, it told him why it haunted that spot.
When the man arranged absolution for this spirit with a priest,
it was freed from its ghostly state and never seen there again.

In another story, a man is attacked at night by a large crow;
sparks flew from its wings as if from a blacksmith's hammer,
but when he drew out his sword and stabbed at the creature,
it seemed as if he struck at a peat-stack. Then it appeared
as a dog with a chain about its neck; looking inside its jaws,
he could see deep into its guts where a furnace was burning.

One ghost came as a bleating goat, turning into a huge man,
horrible-looking, thin as one of the Dead Kings in a painting.
A different Byland spirit *looked like a thorn bush or a bonfire*
one appeared to be *a bullock without a mouth, eyes or ears.*
I know of another which *looked first to be a bull then a cock,
last a white horse: rearing, it seemed to bless with its hooves.*

In a story not included in the Latin original of James' collection,
a ghost came as a bull-headed man to a monk late one night
who thought it a vision of St Luke, evangelist and icon-maker,
as the monk had been illuminating Luke's gospel at that time.
But when it spake, he wrote, *I knew it was no vision of a saint.*
This monk was later burnt for trafficking in demonic knowledge.

Mr Humphreys and His Inheritance

> 'I am son to him that girdeth about the sphere.'
> *Acts of Thomas*, 32.7 (trans. M.R. James)

Written to fill up the volume James wrote
of this tale all false leads and dead-ends,
a Cainite mage and his walled yew maze,
its motto: '*Penetrans Ad Interiora Mortis*'.

Left an estate by an uncle he'd never met,
the hero finds his way to its maze's heart,
to its Gnostic globe with his uncle's ashes.
He maps it that night in the gothic library,

but checking his sketch, at its dead centre
a deep hole begins burning: inside he saw
his uncle's damned soul crawling upwards.
Mr Humphreys is found on the library floor.

That half-rhyme suggests a story tied up –
a box snapping shut in mage Yeats' words.
A coffin shuts on this maze's undead ends
but I am still crawling out of it towards you.

Gnostic Hymn

> 'Anyone who attempts to study according to the ordinary
> and literal sense of the words what Hermetic Philosophers
> write will soon find himself in the twists of a labyrinth.'
>
> *Artephius*

Sophia's crime was giving birth;
she was cast out to walk the Earth,
not here nor there, both near and far
in exile from the Pleroma.

Each country road, each city street
was Sophia's unbeaten path,
her way new ways to know the truth,
new gospels printed by her her feet.

The Demiurge's miscarriage
was all I'd known, the Hell I'd paid,
its womb, the grave where I was laid.
A spark raised me, Sophia's charge.

Though countless nights I'd wandered, lost,
until I found in her my rest;
full dissolution in her flesh
makes mine, my mind and soul afresh.

The edgelands of my mother tongue,
she's my home now, her face, its sky;
her hair gold as my childhood's sun,
her eyes its lapis lazuli.

I see my future in those eyes,
she'll show me when and where to go,
who knows more than the world will know,
who's wise through being otherwise.

Line Please

'A line is: a) a sick circle, b) an unfolded word, c) an aggressive dot, d) what you want to erase, e) what you regret after you dish it out.'
Yoko Ono, *Line Talk*

An aggressive dot stuttering now into morse,
now to Death's autograph on ECG monitors,

the point of this pen ploughing on from birth
to its boring verse-end half-rhyme of death.

What you regret. Inuit rage to Yoruba culture,
lines in land, flesh self-harmed into sculpture;

the trails left by my Oulipian rats in their maze
unravelling like a lie. *What you want to erase:*

those crumpled white sheets as if Cozens' ink
fell like black sunlight on a page I'd wish blank,

its landscape folding under geological strain,
an unfolded word unfolding again and again,

my *sick circle* of mistakes on their Möbius strip,
the repressed returning to read from its script,

my own spirit hesitating on a spiral stairway,
too late for all time with the right thing to say.

Helthwaite

Imagine a city. It is not a city you know,
although it seems familiar as you walk
towards it down a road full of pot-holes
under an arcade of colourless rainbows.

You might try to negotiate the pot-holes
but they are not open to negotiation –
the road only says, take it or leave it.
You turn yet find yourself inside the city.

In deserted avenues of birdless trees,
the houses are implausibly magnificent,
like the ghosts of old-fashioned lunatics
in costumes of long-forgotten fantasies.

All the paving-stones have been stolen,
so you walk down the centre of streets
till one chooses you, its second choice,
you realise, one untaken before now.

Tar glints as if with watchmakers' quartz,
as if you have appointments and are late.
You walk faster, your feet fitting perfectly
the footprints in its dust as thick as snow.

You meet a man wearing black overalls:
he says he's there to paint the gutters
with double-yellow lines, despite a lack
of traffic and the fact his paint is black.

His shadow paints itself into the corner
of your eye, your blind spot. Both wink.
The man assumes an authoritative air,
his glass eye is glinting like the quartz

in the silent watch he presents you with.
It is inscribed with your name and dates,
that it's for your long service to this city.
You weep with pride. Then you just weep.

The Ballad of the Blind Man's Road

When Sterne wrote *Tristram Shandy* back-
to-front and upside-down
and inside-out as Nuttgens' Leeds,
now my home town,

Blind Jack made the road from there
I take to Shandy Hall
so straight and narrow you'd think navvies
men of God and all,

but round Sterne's home folk thought a man
whose impulse was to straighten
showed the signs by ruling lines
of being ruled by Satan.

So like Sterne's book, they made a maze
to leave their fiends behind;
but if they found it hard to leave,
it's harder now to find,

as if a maze outside this maze
held bigger fiends in turn
which tried to keep me from this place
then kept me here to learn.

A railway, just for ghost trains now,
redrew these roads awry
so from Troy maze you can't go west
as if you cannot die.

I thought how Tourneur's film from James
which strayed from what James wrote,
its demon as a railway train,
its straying Coleridge quote:

Like one that on a lonesome road
Doth walk in fear and dread
Because he knows a frightful fiend
Doth close behind him tread.

Still footsteps beating my brain's bounds
may well be only mine,
but past or future I now know
no more than my next line.

Which Reminds Me

for Philippa Troutman

Which reminds me of that time we were digressing
and got lost, going to or from the City of Troy maze,
and a bird swung over the hedge in front of your car,
a female merlin distracted between us and her kill.

Flying slowly before us, she slowed our car down,
as if to see us home or so we could see her home
and we were silent for what seemed like centuries,
held in her mind's claw in lieu of her escaped prey.

Which reminded me of that medieval hunting book,
its raptor hierarchy that gave the merlin to the lady,
which reminded me in turn of Le Roman de Silence,
lost for centuries, anonymous, its narrator unreliable,

its royal lady raised as a male to preserve inheritance,
Silence, disguising herself as a minstrel and a knight,
shapeshifting Merlin only women could trap trapped
by Silence dressed as a man, trapping her in his turn.

Which reminds me of what gets lost in the translation,
or if the *translatio* Silence is, as one critic describes it,
about the writer's relationship to the writing, or if not,
is it a miss like Silence's, our merlin's or this lost plot?

The White Page

> 'Poets don't draw. They unravel their handwriting
> and then tie it up again, but differently. '
>
> *Cocteau*

If you stretch out this writing
into one long, thin single line,
draw it to an invisible thread,

you can make its information
your own material, giving you
the whip-hand over this verse,

this universe, then with a flick
of your wrist, it will ripple into
a silhouette of your own fancy,

a portrait of Widow Wadman
left blank in *Tristram Shandy*
by Sterne for your realisation,

like Botticelli's last white page
for the Virgin in his sequence
illustrating Dante's *Paradiso*,

but even more like Cixous' ink
or letters Molly Bloom sends
herself, love's blind signature.

Lost Chapter

> 'At first each universe was a sort of playground.'
> Philip José Farmer, *Maker of Universes*

Philip José Farmer would trace these mutant lines
to when the Wold Newton Stone had struck Earth
on the grounds of the real son of imaginary Didius,
who launched Sterne's writing career as the target
of the pulped History of a Good Warm Watch-Coat,
as the groundbreaking meteorite targeted this Wold
to explode the Ptolemaic model of our solar system,
freeing up scientists to launch their own astronomies
as Farmer launched a Wold Newton Universe Family,
connecting descendants of passengers on coaches
passing ground zero, their *nova of genetic splendour*
charted by Farmer down to such as Sherlock Holmes,
Lecoq, Laboeuf, Monk Mayfair, Bloom, the Shadow,
to our mutant hero hobby horse Trismegistus Brandy,
Trismegistus for 'Thrice Great' as Yorkshire Ridings,
Brandy a double-distillation (as poetry to Connolly)
of postilion cocktail horses on the passing coaches,
Brandy now wondering, not at his genetic splendour,
but how to escape the labyrinth of this first sentence,
when he recalled a turn from Virgil, the *Ludus Trojae*
and with a single bound he was as free as this verse.

Brandy shivered, caught his breath and looked about.
Gifted with ninja mutant hero powers of camouflage,
he drifted invisibly through villages around Coxwold,
hiding as a hobby horse, a morris dancers' costume,
his coat blackening into shadows as if silver nitrate.
He grazed cottage bookshelves while humans slept,
devouring all kinds of book like oats from a nosebag.
But tonight, Brandy dines on Shandy Hall's library
reading about Gargantua's love of his hobby horses,

changing their coats as monks changed dalmatics.
He disliked Burton's gibe *fed horses and town bulls*
but knew Hoffman's Tomcat Murr was a kindred spirit,
loving Cervantes, not for Don Quixote, but Rocinante,
Rocín meaning a cheap horse like his family cocktail.
Brandy wanted to be a hero unsaddled by any knight.
He imagined taking the Kilburn Mouseman for a page.
Page Brandy repeated, *Page, Pages, Pegasus, Jesus*...

As Sterne inhaled infections here, hallucinogenic spores
from mildewed pages invaded Brandy's lungs and blood.
Soon, he felt stabbing pains in his side. His head ached.
When he coughed, he saw sparks behind his shut eyes.
Words on this page melted to suminagashi *ink floating*
when he tried to read them, then it everything went black.
He dreamt he read his own name on the spines of books,
row upon row: his life and opinions filled the whole library.
He took one down to find a paper knife between its pages
marking a picture of himself as Wicked Knife's white mare
from The Maker of Universes. He flicked through the book,
which made a whirring sound. He was in all of its pictures,
selves jostling in the book like watch-coats in a wardrobe,
and Brandy changed them as Gargantua his hobby horses:
now a bullring lancer's mount, now the lancer, now the bull.
Then he was a customer in a coaching inn ordering a round
and being asked by its barman why he had such a long face.
Outside, a coach-owner cursed the new paint job on its door,
a bend dexter rendered sinister, a coat of arms back-to-front,
just back from where the Wold Stone had struck like a clock.
Running down the chapters of its face, Brandy could now see
the Kilburn Mouseman fleeing from Philip José Farmer's wife
brandishing a knife pulled from between the pages of a book
like the sword from the stone. The clock whirred, set to strike–

Brandy woke up hearing turbine blades from the wind farm.
He imagined them hoisting Don Quixote from Rocinante
as he tried to hoist his dream from his unconscious mind
but managed only fragments of its wild and whirling words:

...I am the celestial meteor...Two coach-horses a-breast...
poetry and prose are one...language the old shapeshifter...
your hobby horse is running away with you...Oh Murr, Murr
Brandy murmured, aware he was losing something unique,
like that coach chapter so good Sterne cut it from his book.
Brandy knew all authors targeted innocent, misplaced ideas,
taking a knife to those they knew were special like Isaacs,
the root of whose name, Brandy now recalled, was laughter.
As a mutant, he felt kinship with the Murdered Darling family
and finding their Neverland would be an awfully big adventure;
he need only take control of this hybrid vehicle and take off,
stardust to the stars like Cornelia Parker's dream meteorite,
night and day his inkwell and palette. Brandy looked down
at the bottom of this page as white as his coat with promise,
looked up at the sky twinkling back. And then it struck him.

Notes and acknowledgements

We are grateful to Arts Council England for funding the Digressions project, Chris Pearson and Patrick Wildgust at Shandy Hall, Maura Dooley and especially Claire Malcolm of New Writing North, for her crucial support, encouragement and imagination.

A number of these poems, or some very like them, have already appeared elsewhere. Thanks are therefore due to the editors of *Poetry Review*, *Poetry* (US), *Edinburgh Review*, *Canto*, *Compose* (US), *Poetry & Audience*, *The Lifeboat* (Belfast), *The Critical Muslim*, *The Dark Horse*.

'Li Xiaodong's Maze' was written for the launch of the Sensing Spaces exhibition at the Royal Academy in January 2014, appearing in an anthology with the name *Sensing Spaces: Wandering Words* (Ekphrasis, 2014).

'The Marbled Page' was written for a Shandy Hall project called *The Emblem of My Work* and appeared in the Laurence Sterne Trust exhibition and 2013 catalogue of that name.

Afterforeword

Why *Afterforeword*? Well, I felt this was a hybrid of a foreword and afterword, coming up with this Germanic-sounding compound as a solution. I suspected so much prose before the body of poetry and art here would deter some readers, while I hope those interested by the foregoing may continue their investigations here. It is also true that the making of *Digressions* has been in many ways a paradoxical process, not least because in *Tristram Shandy,* Sterne introduces us to a paradoxical world, reversing many of a reader's expectations; regarding *Tristram Shandy*, Horace Walpole wrote 'the great humour of which consists in the whole narration always going backwards', and though its chronology might suggest this from time, its structure is nowhere near as simple as that. Furthermore, the novel itself can be viewed as having risen from the dead, Samuel Johnson famously declaring it deceased in his lifetime: 'Nothing odd will do long. *Tristram Shandy* did not last.' The corpse went on to show much greater vigour than the doctor and it is healthier than ever today.

Bearing that in mind, where should we begin? You'll notice, should you visit Shandy Hall, a framed and mounted Krauze cartoon from Stuart Kelly's *The Book of Lost Books*. This shows a copy of *Tristram Shandy* carved into the shape of a maze, an appropriate emblem for the course of the *Digressions* project, which began to take its labyrinthine shape at the end of 2013, the Tercentenary of Sterne's birth. Like Gaul and Yorkshire, *Digressions* is divided into three parts: poetry, art and prose, appearing both in this book and magazines, on the internet and at exhibitions scheduled for Yorkshire and London, as well as travelling events on a smaller scale that are a mixture of these. To a certain extent, this tripartite division reflects Horace Walpole's claim that 'Poetry, Painting, and Gardening, or the science of Landscape, will be forever by men of Taste deemed Three Sisters, or the Three New Graces who dress and adorn Nature'; although we hope that our Sisters will appeal to women of Taste as well, we couldn't pretend to be adorning Nature, and certainly not in God's Own County, as its natives are pleased to call it, where my Gardening will take the form of pointing at neglected places within its landscape in a kind of knock-off John Baldessari exhibition.

I've always liked the notion of a 'riding' as a measure, an unusually dynamic unit which here and now puts me in mind Frost's analogy for a poem's course as ice riding its own dissolution. *Digressions* was measured out by the ridings of my string of hobby horses and the melting of forms. The only other place I have personally come across in these islands divided into ridings is Tipperary, where Sterne (and my father) were born and there is an Irish dimension, among many others, to *Digressions*. Although he himself could display virulent anti-Catholicism and use the adjective 'Irish' as a term of abuse in the ecclesiastical and political disputes he became caught up in, it is worth bearing in mind that he lived through the very real Catholic threat of the Jacobite rising under the Young Pretender. There is a very real military dimension to Sterne, a soldier's son, in his life and work, and it is one that is also reflected in *Digressions*. On the question of his bigotry, nevertheless, it is important to remember that Sterne spoke out for the victims of the slave trade at a time when it was neither fashionable nor advantageous for him to do so. In 1766, Ignatius Sancho wrote to Sterne asking him to write something against slavery, encouraged by a passage he read in Sterne's sermons, which had recently appeared as *The Sermons of Mr Yorick*. Sterne replied to Sancho and kept copies of the letters. We will return later to what Sterne wrote responding to this in *Tristram Shandy*.

A vaguely racist undertone lingers in a popular usage word 'Irish' as I am going to invoke it to reclaim it here, meaning quaint, paradoxical, back-to-front, as in the phrase 'That's very Irish of you', employed when the speaker has uttered something in apparent contradiction of common sense, for example in Mahaffey's explanation of an 'Irish bull' (an expression related to 'a cock and bull story') when he said 'An Irish bull is always pregnant'. In this peculiar linguistic sense, it could be said that *Tristram Shandy* is one of the most Irish novels ever written. However, I'd go further in justification of the Irish dimension of

Digressions by pointing to Sterne's real literary influence on significant Irish writers such as James Joyce and Flann O'Brien especially in the latter's novel *The Third Policeman*, where hobby horses are updated into bicycles in a world of circular wanderings.

Of course, *Tristram Shandy*'s influence was felt throughout Europe as well as in the Anglophone countries – in Russia, for example on Pushkin, while the novel's discovery by the Russian Formalists in the 1920s gave it a new lease of life there. Shklovsky analysed *Tristram Shandy* as being structured around digressions sabotaging narrative momentum to a principle that he called 'retardation'. However, I was more particularly taken with the playfulness of one German response to *Tristram Shandy*, Hoffman's *The Life and Opinions of Tomcat Murr*, where the composer and author almost out-Shandies Sterne in his crazy inventiveness. In this book, the eponymous feline has written his prose and poetry on the back of what he considers to be waste paper, in fact Johannes Kreisler's story, in the process confusing and reversing our reading time in that narrative of the archetypal Romantic Kreisler, whose name invokes '*Kreis*' meaning circle. Murr is even involved in some of the same play of identities shown in *Tristram Shandy*, for example in Volume VII Chapter 33: 'as sure as I am I and you are you – and who are you? said he. – Don't puzzle me; said I.' In Part 1 of *The Life and Opinions of Tomcat Murr,* he muses, 'I then fell into a state that, dividing my Self in a curious way from my Self, yet seemed to be my *real* self.' Passages like this seem especially contemporary given our modern interrogation of the lyric I and the persistence of the Ego in literary criticism. Sterne carried these games into real life when in London he could move between being Sterne, Tristram and Yorick. This is like a playful version of the fate of thieves in Dante's *Inferno* who, because they made no distinction between '*meum*' and '*tuum*', lose even their stable egos. The issue of theft brings calls up a very present concern with plagiarism, especially in the world of poetry, by which I don't mean Détournement, or the use of appropriated texts by Conceptual writers in new ways, but passing off other people's work as your own to win prizes in competitions or gain publication kudos (a digression I don't have time to pursue would involve an analysis of gender power relationships in this area and why these kinds of plagiarists seem to be all male, even though they frequently steal women's writings). Of a very different nature is what lies behind *Tristram Shandy*'s histrionic denunciation of plagiarism – itself plagiarised from Burton's *The Anatomy of Melancholy*.

A tune is a hobby horse that can be ridden by lyrics with very different allegiances in a practice we can trace from medieval contrafacta to modern football chants. However, here I am as much concerned with the character of the tune. I wrote an article once for *Poetry Ireland Review* connecting Irish song styles with the narrative techniques of Sterne, Paul Muldoon and Flann O'Brien, among others, quoting Samuel P. Bayard:

'The English singer's leaning to relatively straightforward and simple melodic lines is counteracted in Irish tradition by a love of ornament, of multiplying notes, of varying rhythmic patterns by this sort of multiplication. This ornamental tendency gives Irish music a 'wavering and unemphatic movement' as opposed to the English preference for the sort of melodic movement that 'gets somewhere', while the Irish habit of lingering on certain notes and tones, 'repeating them before going on to another tone, thus almost impeding the onward course of the melody… dwelling on inconclusive or indecisive scale-tones that do not contribute to resolution or finality in the entire phrase or musical utterance…' For all the world, this sounds very much like Shklovsky's principle of retardation applied to Irish singing.

Researching *Digressions* involved consideration of, and discoveries in, not only historical texts, but many at the very forefront of contemporary experimental poetry. A number of authors who have held residencies at Shandy Hall are of international standing in the field of Conceptual writing, such as Kenneth Goldsmith, Craig Dworkin and Christian Bök. I could not fail to find Conceptual writing interesting, not least as it appears in part to be a hybrid of art and literature as Sterne frequently referred to what he was doing in *Tristram Shandy* as 'painting'. I decided that if I got the opportunity to do something sustained with *Tristram Shandy*, I should set up an artist's mirror opposite my own to multiply the creative reflections that would become available. When Arts Council of England funding made it possible, I immediately thought of Philippa Troutman. I have enjoyed her own work for many years and responded to some of it in my last book Pandorama, which contains a sequence based on her travelling exhibition *The Shanties*, developed from her research into the lives of the railway navvies and their families, and the horrors they suffered during the building of the Ribblehead Viaduct. Her sense of place was important, as I wanted the real place of Shandy Hall, Coxwold village and its countryside to anchor what I was trying to do in space and time, however those categories might be fluid. Wallace Stevens wrote that we do not live in places but in the descriptions of places and I was keen to incorporate new renditions of locality in *Digressions* beyond the verbal. However, beyond any notion of her sensitivity place and history, Philippa is a very versatile, contemporary and experimental artist. For example, I quickly saw the value of her cut-ups of *Tristram Shandy*'s text: apart from being visually interesting, they developed its theme of accident and we called Sortes Shandeanae, 'Shandean Lots', on the analogy of 'Virgilian Lots', although I don't recommend it as a predictive tool. In printmaking, she introduced me not only to a great range of techniques, but also to accidents of the process such as 'foul bite', where acid strays into and affects unintended areas of the metal, full of intellectual reverberations in relation to place and trespass in society and genres of art. A reference in a book I read during this time, *Printmaking Today* by Jules Heller, seemed particularly relevant:

> The Printmaker is a most peculiar being. He (sic) delights in deferred gratification and in doing what does not come naturally. He takes pleasure in working backward or in opposites: the gesture that produces a line of force moving to the right prints to the left, and vice versa; a deeply engraved trench in a copper or zinc plate prints as a depression in the paper. Left is right. Right is left. Backward is forward. The Printmaker, peculiar as he is, must see at least two sides to every question.

Philippa also introduced me to suminagashi ('floating ink') marbling techniques added new dimensions to my understanding of these processes, which I had some acquaintance with having contributed to Shandy Hall's *The Emblem of My Work* exhibition of 2013, inspired by *Tristram Shandy*'s marbled page. In one style of suminagashi, Japanese court artists sought to let ink on prepared paper immersed in the marbling trough to dissolve and create new patterns on the surface of the liquid, parallel to processes we were engaged in, immersing the text of *Tristram Shandy* in new media, seeing how its ink drifted smokily, reconstituting itself into new meanings. Alternatively, in the more usual suminagashi technique, where ink is dripped onto the surface of the liquid, its growing enclosed spheres reminded me of the matryoshka worlds of the Ptolemaic cosmic model destroyed by the Wold Newton meteorite, which I will return to shortly. Ptolemy's tiered and broken worlds also reflected the science fiction Wold Newton Universe created by Philip José Farmer, another new discovery entering the creative mix after I chanced upon his writings. Philippa's flexibility with techniques and approaches was a perfect foil for me for investigating Sterne's motley novel in different settings.

Motley, things being various, hybrid and becoming each other in the world I was investigating led me to be particularly struck by a passage in Matthew Sperling's excellent new book *Visionary Philology: Geoffrey Hill and the Study of Words*. Interpreting poem 20 of *Speech! Speech!* where Hill writes 'you wriggle so, / old shape-shifter', Sperling interestingly comments 'Language itself, therefore, is the "old shape-shifter"'. Hill's *Mercian Hymns* hadn't been long published when I started as a student at Leeds University in 1974 where Hill was working at the time and it is one of his collections I have a special affection for as a result. Among other aspects of the book, I liked the way Offa as presiding genius passed through time and space and modes of address, and this was certainly in my mind while writing *Digressions,* although I was working at a less serious level, in the sense that I wanted a Shandean spirit to permeate the landscape as well as my words.

I read Sperling's book at the same time as I was studying the ghost stories collected by a monk from Byland Abbey in the Middle Ages, which M.R. James brought to the attention of a wider public at the beginning of the last century. These tales often had Christian morals tacked on to Scandinavian patterns, for the Viking penetration of Yorkshire went very deep indeed, linguistically as well as imaginatively. When I was at Leeds University, its English Department hosted research into the *Dialect Atlas of Great Britain*, where I learned, for example, as we keep returning to the notion of 'play' here, that the Yorkshire word '*laikin*', meaning playing, was etymologically related to the name of the child's toy Lego. The terror of the Byland tales reside not so much in what the ghosts do as in the flux of their being, not just from human to animal, but from living matter into inanimate objects, much like the fate of the thief in Dante's *Inferno*. In M.R. James' short story *Mr Humphreys and His Inheritance*, the suggestion is made that the soul of Humphrey's damned uncle is transmuted into an Irish yew. For some reason, I identified this yew with the tree that fell in a storm enabling Byland Abbey to be seen from Shandy Hall.

A maze plays a central part in this M.R. James story and planning digressions around Shandy Hall I read about some interesting-sounding local mazes. Alerted by Chris Pearson at Shandy Hall, Philippa and I attempted to visit one of them, Asenby's Maiden's Bower. I met Philippa for the Asenby trip in Ripon and took the opportunity to Shandy about in Market Place while I waited for her. In places like that, I see dead people: its witch-smellers, wife-sellers and Catholic recusants gathered for the disastrous Rising of the North. Appleton's Butchers is still there, its sausages so gorgeous Naomi Jacob described them as 'poems in skins', not to be brutally stabbed by a fork on the frying pan but pierced with a darning needle. This reminded me of Tomcat Murr's description of books with mixed poems and prose, where he opines that the former should be like lumps of bacon in a sausage, to be discovered with a special glee – which only goes to show that this modern fashion of presenting a 'sausage' as a collapsed pattie betrays its very essence; the content and the form have a vital interdependence as with a poem, be it subject to Oulipian constraint or the rules governing villanelles.

On arrival at the site of the Asenby maze, located behind the Crab and Lobster pub according to our information, the landlord told me he'd never heard of it, which I found hard to believe. On further investigation outside, as I stumbled about like a lost minotaur looking for its maze, half Irish bull, we discovered the mound on which the maze was supposed to be located was now part of a miniature or 'crazy golf' course. Sorry that such a feature of topographical interest had been lost in this way, I comforted myself by remembering that 'Shandy' used to mean 'crazy' and imagining what Shandean golf might be like, with bunkers including Toby and Trim's military earthworks and holes missing, in the wrong order, or subject to metaphysical speculation with double entendres about holes being deployed in battalions.

Philippa and I did, however, on another expedition eventually manage to find the City of Troy, coiled on its hillside like a Cumberland sausage, a humble piece of land art with that magnificent, legendary name. Modest though it is, and I understand it to be the smallest such maze in Europe, this turf mandala which never seems to appear on maps is a perfect location for 'bewilderment' in Fanny Howe's sense: a site physically reflecting the spirals of poetry in its structures of repetition and refrain, like Bayard's Irish music or those ancient recurring spirals Jorn described in his unrealised *10,000 Years of Nordic Folk Art*. The circular mazes of Jerusalem Miles in cathedrals were supposed to replace an actual pilgrimage, but our actual pilgrimages resembled entering the labyrinth of a Jerusalem Mile after we set off from from Leeds on shuttling journeys over the life of *Digressions*.

Leeds is a paradoxical place in itself, its name sounding a pun full of promise to the seeker while being 'completely outside the literary world' according to the former editor of *Granta*, John Freeman. The architectural historian Patrick Nuttgens titled his 1979 book about the place *Leeds: the Back to Front Inside Out Upside Down City* and in its opening sentences wrote 'The first and most constant problem with the City of Leeds is to find it.

There never was a more faceless city or a more deceptive one. It hasn't a face because it has too many faces, all of them different; it's a city without logical unity.' Perfect, therefore, as a springboard for launching an investigation into a Shandean world. I'm not a native, and it always has been a focus for immigration, with significant Irish, Caribbean, African and Jewish communities. This has made it a target of prejudice and regarding the last of these groups it has attracted anti-Semitic nicknames which include the Holy City and the Jerusalem of the North–paradoxical abuse, you might think, for an old Puritan town. Leeds' Jewish communities centred formerly on Chapeltown, and we'd take the Chapeltown Road where live to get to Ripon, Shandy Hall and our other digressions including the City of Troy, a road I found out was made by a blind man, Jack Metcalf. Metcalf was building roads at the same time that Sterne was writing *Tristram Shandy*, and it seemed significant in itself that a blind man should make the straight road I took to get lost in Sterne's labyrinthine novel and our network of *Digressions* from and around Coxwold including the maze of Troy.

After having photographed, made notes on and sketched the City of Troy, we discovered that leaving it is even more difficult than finding it. It is possible to drive north or south from there, not easy to drive east and impossible to drive due west, a bit like a version of Abbott's *Lineland* but gathering ancient mythical associations of being cut off from the land of the dead in the direction of the sunset. I'm assuming this difficulty in the roads is something to do with the long-gone railway line; I'd noticed the Coxwold signal-box at the bottom of the village, now there only for ghost trains or 'trains of ideas', as Locke describes them, which complicate so enrichingly the narrative of *Tristram Shandy*. I felt as if the imaginary train had been conflated with the fiend at the end of Jacques Tourneur's *Night of the Demon*, which was pursuing me from Troy because, like it, I was too much a creature of the straight line. Film as a medium was much in my mind while working on *Digressions*, perhaps because of Michael Winterbottom's achievement in his film *A Cock and Bull Story*, a paradoxically successful version of what most people would regard as the essentially unfilmable *Tristram Shandy* achieved by foregrounding those very problems, among other means. I've often thought that film is closer to poetry than prose as both rely on successions of images, while the non-Shandean novel, in Eudora Welty's phrase must attend to the mechanics of getting people in and out of rooms. Rebecca Solnit, in another book I recommend, her *A Field Guide to Getting Lost*, uses the physical image of film-strip for an Ariadne thread, especially apposite in this context, while Patrick Keiller in *The View From The Train* writes 'Films even physically resemble railway tracks – long, parallel sided strips divided laterally by frame lines and perforations, as is the railway by sleepers.' Straight roads and railway tracks are what busy city people want, not to mention developing capitalism – Patrick Keiller has made the Wold Newton Meteorite a harbinger of deracinated mobile labour exploited through the Speenhamland System. This puts me in mind of how in *Das Kapital* Marx's biographer Francis Wheen sees the influence of Sterne, making that work, like *Tristram Shandy*, 'full of systems and syllogisms, paradoxes and metaphysics, theories and hypotheses, abstruse explanations and whimsical tomfoolery.'

I quoted Wallace Stevens earlier and here invoke his definition 'A poem is a meteor'. I think his idea was that they consume themselves with their own fire, rather like Frost's ice poem which rides its own melting that I invoked earlier. If part of them make it to Earth, they become even more laden with symbolism – Wolfram Von Eschenbach's grail was a meteorite, for example. The area around Shandy Hall is historically rich with them and meteorites have a particular appeal now to artists such as Cornelia Parker and Patrick Keiller. When I had the opportunity to discuss them with Cornelia Parker, she mentioned her ambition to relaunch one into space, which seems an appropriately paradoxical and Shandean thing to do. At a literally more mundane level, Patrick Keiller included the Wold Cottage Stone in his Robinson Institute in the context already mentioned, but it has always had a particularly Shandean significance for me. I first came across it, as paradigm-shattering in its scientific sphere as *Tristram Shandy* was in literature, in the course of reading Roger Osborne's *A Floating Egg: Episodes in the Making of Geology*. Osborne describes how it landed on the grounds of Edward Topham in Wold Newton, and quotes Topham's letter to the Oracle newspaper published on 12th February 1796:

> At Bridlington, and at different villages, sounds were heard in the air, which the inhabitants took to be the noise of guns at sea; but at two adjoining villages, the noise was so distinct of something singular passing through the air towards my habitation, that five or six people came up to see if anything extraordinary had happened to my house or grounds. In burying itself in the earth it threw up a greater quantity of soil than a shell would, and to a much greater extent. When the labourer recovered from the extreme alarm into which the descent of such a Stone had thrown him, his first description was, 'that the clouds opened as it fell, and he thought HEAVEN and EARTH were coming together!

Edward Topham is only one of the fascinating characters I stumbled upon during the Digressions project. He was the son of the model for Sterne's Didius, Francis Topham, who first propelled the author into a literary career with his *The Adventures of a Watch-Coat* (Didius also appears in *Tristram Shandy*) directed at Francis, who had attempted to secure for Edward the living of Sutton-in-the-Forest at York. The boy Edward led the famous 1768 boys' revolt at Eton but later, joining the army, he earned the gratitude of the King by clearing Parliament Square during the anti-Catholic Gordon Riots. He later founded the most scurrilous and successful paper of his day, The World, during his tenure there establishing the limits of the laws of libel, setting the precedent that the dead cannot be libelled. Returning to Yorkshire as a magistrate, he took up dog-racing and bred one of the most famous greyhounds in history, Snowball–with appropriate paradox for our theme, a black dog.

However, getting back to the significance of his meteorite, it far transcends the literary, requiring a new scientific understanding of such phenomena: Humphry Davy's address on taking the chair for his first ordinary meeting of the Royal

Society as President includes the passage on 'meteors which, in passing through our atmosphere, throw down showers of stones; for it cannot be doubted that they belong to the heavens, and that they are not fortuitous or atmospheric formations', it having previously been imagined that such astronomical traffic was impossible due to the legacy of a Ptolemaic model of our solar system and that meteorites were the result of volcanic eruptions sending matter into the atmosphere that then fell back to earth. This paradigm shift necessitated considerable adjustment in some quarters, Thomas Jefferson supposedly declaring 'It is easier to believe that Yankee professors would lie rather than that stones would fall from Heaven.' The phenomenon stirred later American imaginations though as the event founded a whole school of US science fiction writing, the Wold Newton Family centred around the work of Philip José Farmer. Farmer's conceit was that passing coach passengers included pregnant women who were radioactively affected by the meteorite at the genetic level so their descendants ultimately included the likes of Sherlock Holmes' adversary Moriarty, H.G. Wells' Time Traveller, Allan Quatermain, Doc Savage, Tarzan, Raffles, and Leopold Bloom – not the only appearance of Joyce in Farmer's oeuvre: his 1967 novella, *Riders of the Purple Wage* is a pastiche of *Finnegans Wake*. That Farmer is keen on unlikely crossover figures can be deduced from the title of another of his books, *Jesus on Mars*. I knew I should maintain a sensitivity to the Christian dimensions of Sterne's work but I hadn't imagined it would take me to the Red Planet.

Having found so much of interest flowing from the Wold Newton Meteorite, a trip to Byland Abbey and the nearby Kilburn White Horse with Philippa was also attractive because of the history of the Hambleton Meteorite, a pallasite discovered near there in 2005, in relation to which I was very interested to come across a widely-held view now that it is a remnant of the Great Meteor of 1783, the year of a major edition of Sterne's life and works (there is a copy in Shandy Hall library). One unlikely report of the Great Meteor contained in a contemporary issue of *The London Magazine* concerns an officer's account as seen from his warship moored off Ireland, which mentions it stopping and reversing before continuing its former course, a very Sternean thing for it to do. So I Shandied about in Google for 1783 to see what other Sternean things were going on and discovered it to be the year of a stage version of *Tristram Shandy* as 'a bagatelle in two acts'. This adaptation was by the Dublin barrister Leonard McNally, and 'a sentimental and jingoistic celebration of British military might' according to Oakley in *A Culture of Mimicry*. McNally's legal writings fixed the standard of criminal prosecution at *beyond reasonable doubt*; as well as a playwright, he was a lyricist most famous for *The Sweet Lass of Richmond Hill*. McNally was a founder member of the United Irishmen, betraying them systematically to the Crown at every stage through to offering to act as defence counsel for its leaders after the failure of the 1798 Rising (which McNally did so much to bring about), ensuring their convictions by secretly cooperating with the prosecution. I contacted Donald MacRaild, Professor of British and Irish History at the University of Ulster, about McNally, who as you can imagine is neither popular with the Irish or the English, to try and gain some insight into his motives. Money, Donald said. Britain was one of the richest countries in the world then and paid vast sums in today's terms to maintain its security on its vulnerable Irish flank. I didn't have more time on the *Digressions* project to digress further into the story McNally, but there is surely room for other writers to do so. Famous in his day, vilified by all sides since his treachery emerged after his death, McNally's star fell into complete obscurity.

That Sterne's name puns on the German for star was ingeniously deployed by contributors to Shandy Hall's *Black Page* exhibition of 2009, which reminded me of an old love poem with the lines *'Du bist mein Glück, Du bist mein Stern.'* '*Glück*' puts me in mind of how luck, chance, accident and design obsessed Sterne as a religious man whose faith in a divinely-ordained universe is inevitably compromised by their existence, as Fortuna was such a theologically questionable character to the medieval Church. The role of chance in modern art, however, has become something of a fetish. I was always struck by the unlikely story often told about finding a name for dada (its hobby horse meaning already connecting it with *Tristram Shandy* in my mind) by randomly sliding a knife into a dictionary. The blade's meteoric intrusion into the world of letters is made in this way to appear part of a grander design than merely thinking up a name or reclaiming an insult, the work of an artistic Blind Watchmaker, or more appropriately in the Shandean universe, a Blind Clockmaker.

At Leeds University, one of my art lecturers was Sir Lawrence Gowing, who announced authoritatively in a lecture on Alexander Cozens of the famous blot-and-paper-crumpling landscape technique that there is no such thing as chance in art: Cozens' crumpling of paper was analogous to the folding of geological strata while the apparently random fall of ink within it recreated the fall of light and shadow on and from rock. Nevertheless, I thought, isn't there a genuine element of chance brought about by the resistance of the medium if nothing else? Every poet knows the feeling that she is only being allowed to take particular directions with her writing because of the nature of the language, especially when trying to box the shadows of rhyme: 'Words mean something because they always threaten to sound like something else' James Longenbach wrote in *The Art of the Poetic Line*. The delusion persists that 'It rhymes for a reason', as the saying goes, which it obviously doesn't, though a poet may work hard to give the impression that it does. Perhaps the habitual effort to square circles is one of the things that distinguishes the artist from the scientist, although in his old age Thomas Hobbes convinced himself that he had actually managed to achieve this geometrical feat.

Francis Bacon (perhaps coming to mind after thinking of Murr's comments about sausages) described something like this in an interview: 'In my case all painting... is an accident. I foresee it and yet I hardly ever carry it out as I foresee it. It transforms itself by the actual paint.' And again, 'All painting is an accident. But it's also not an accident, because one must select what part of the accident one chooses to preserve' and in a demonstration of the practical artist's eat-your-cake-and-have-it approach, 'I want a very ordered image, but I want it to come about by chance.' I don't believe this argument will ever be settled, an aesthetic equivalent of the Arian controversy about the nature of divine precedence within the Trinity, where the terms of the debate eventually become irrelevant. However, I was reading something by Rachel Galvin in *The Boston Review* recently where she referred to 'Oulipian writers who are anti-Chance', reminding me of the suspiciously-convenient story of dada obtaining its name from a paper knife slid between the pages of a dictionary. This too seemed to demonstrate Bacon's desire for a very ordered image brought about by chance, the hobby horse flushed from linguistic cover to be the Pegasus for machine-age artists. But the machine we are mostly ghosts in now is intangible itself: 'The Internet is a giant machine that does nothing but generate writing' was a recent Tweet from Kenneth Goldsmith. Goldsmith makes the Internet sound like the Tarot was to Italo Calvino and regards Tweets as Oulipian constraints generating a kind of poetry he calls poetweets. For Raymond Queneau, Oulipo's co-founder, Oulipians are 'Rats who build the labyrinth from which they will try to escape', which sounds to me like the attitudes to chance of Bacon and whoever devised the dada story about its name: it should be fairly easy to find your way out of the labyrinth you build yourself after all. Sterne writes about *Tristram Shandy* as a machine at the beginning of the first chapter of Volume VII, but at a superficial level it appears to be one jury-rigged with bolted-on features back-to-front, made from whatever came to hand as a hedge-carpenter might effect rough and ready repairs from whatever lumber was about.

The internet is the modern writer's lumber yard, but another writer concerned with the implications of religion has a more negative view of the Internet, which he thinks his absence from enhances serendipity: in his recent Oxford lecture, Geoffrey Hill said 'Because I don't go online in any way, I think and work almost entirely by serendipity. Serendipity works by the rule that the book which is to change your life stands next on the shelf to the book that you had intended to take out from the library, and which as often as not (the book you had wanted I mean) turns out to be a dud. You must envisage me, then, reading and writing from the centre of a small intense radiance of apprehension, a miniature vortex of intuition.' Ironies here include that the lecture is available online, but you know what he means.

In the absence of a better word, I often ended up using '*desearch*' in talks about the *Digressions* project to describe the process that led me to McNally, for example: a semi-organised serendipity that you could could still not describe by the more purposeful word research. The book that stands next on the shelf to the book that Geoffrey Hill intends to get but turns out more valuable to him is, nevertheless, on that shelf according to the principles of a non-serendipitous classification system. Some other practice is required to thwart the demons of efficiency; even second hand bookshops can be too organised for such purposes and even some charity bookshops such as Oxfam present their stock in well-ordered sections. I don't know if Queneau's rats were in the back of my mind when I decided to buy Nick Mays' book on the care of fancy rats, a creature I've never kept. The National Fancy Rat Society, whose history Mays traces in passing, struck me as such a wonderful example of hobbyhorsicality that I attended one of their events in Bradford. Tremendous love and care was lavished on these rats, which I discovered would laugh when they were tickled, like their owners looking down warmly on them as they did so, putting me in mind of the notion that people are supposed to start resembling their pets in a process analogous to that described by Sterne whereby our prolonged contact with our hobby horses leads to an interchange of natures. Flann O'Brien took this idea further in *The Third Policeman* through the book's version of 'atomic theory', with this hybridisation an actual physical process at the molecular level between riders and their bicycles and all this not unlike the idea of joined beings taking place during the ceremonial coronation rite of sexual intercourse between Irish kings and horses Gerald of Wales recounts in his *Topographica Hibernica*, which I need hardly say is historically controversial, especially in Ireland. Nevertheless, when I was working on a commission to update the fourteenth century Fauvel cycle for the Clerks Group about the usurping horse-king in a world turned upside-down by Dame Fortuna's wheel, I was fascinated to read Emma Dillon in her *Medieval Music-Making and the*

demonically straight, but taking in its byways: following Sterne is a paradoxical pun on his name in itself about chasing tails and often reminded me of something Blake wrote, 'Improvement makes straight roads, but the crooked roads, without improvement, are roads of Genius.'

Sometimes the language in *Tristram Shandy* doesn't move at all but disappears, as in its missing chapters, black and marbled pages, the murdered darling of the coach journey or when, to describe the beauty of Widow Wadman, the readers' imaginations are directly commissioned by Sterne with a blank page: 'paint her to your own mind' which calls to my mind Botticelli's climactic blank page for his illustrations to *The Divine Comedy*. The white space we have arrived at isn't Dante's '*candida rosa*' but Yorkshire's White Rose, whose culture and country we invite you to enjoy, to 'Shandy about' in, to use Sterne's phrase; a strange land of tangled songlines, its anthem, *On Ilkla Moor Baht'at*, seeming to invoke the worms of *Hamlet* as *Tristram Shandy* constantly invokes this play about the fatal retardation of its hero's actions. While Yorick lives again for Sterne, Hamlet dies uttering 'The rest is silence' just before the thunderous applause of audiences everywhere throughout time. The rest is nearly silence here too: our final Yorkshire paradox is to welcome you by saying get lost. *Digressions* is our record of just how rewarding a process that can be.

Ian Duhig,
Leeds, 2014

Roman de Fauvel how in handling its manuscript in the Bibliothèque nationale de France, 'as flesh meets flesh, skin mingles with skin... readers, also, literally, become part of the object.' In this case it is human skin touching the animal skin of medieval vellum.

Touching the skins of rats to make them laugh or, to make me laugh again, the calfskin binding of 1783 Sterne's Life and Works in the Shandy Hall library (the year of the Great Meteor); touching the skin of an Appleton's sausage, testing the poetry inside–but these actions touch on abuse too: harm is done to creatures routinely on an industrial scale to provide us with food, especially fast food. Such considerations led to my wife and son to become vegetarians and me to do my best in that direction as well. Harm is done to humans too, historically, treating them like animals for reasons that are no more than skin deep or to do with gender. I alluded at the beginning of this to Sterne's opposition to slavery, and there is an affecting episode in *Tristram Shandy*, written in response to the letter from Ignatius Sancho where the abuse of a black serving girl who works in a sausage shop is described, and the following exchange between Trim and Uncle Toby takes place:

Why then, an' please your honour, is a black wench to be used worse than a white one?
I can give no reason, said my Uncle Toby –
– Only, cried the corporal, shaking his head, because she has no one to stand up for her.

This still has the power to stop the reader in her tracks as it did me when I first read the book: it alerts us to a moral dimension to our consumption. The Slow Food movement emerged in the 1980s as a critique of Western society, growing from opposition to McDonald's, and then everything that chain symbolised. Slow Reading emerged from this, although some trace the phrase back to Nietzsche, who referred to himself as a teacher of slow reading. In a 2009 *Guardian* article, Nick Laird stated 'To read poetry now is to be part of a Slow Language Movement.' Books like *Tristram Shandy* require us to read slowly, never